How to Succeed in Geometry

Grades 3-5

Editors
Polly Hoffman
Gisela Lee

Editorial Manager
Karen J. Goldfluss, M.S. Ed.

Editor-in-Chief
Sharon Coan, M.S. Ed.

Cover Artist
Jessica Orlando

Art Coordinator
Kevin Barnes

Creative Director
CJae Froshay

Imaging
Rosa C. See
Alfred Lau

Product Manager
Phil Garcia

Acknowledgements
Word® software is © 1983–2000
Microsoft Corporation. All
rights reserved. Word is a
registered trademark of
Microsoft Corporation.

Publishers
Rachelle Cracchiolo, M.S. Ed.
Mary Dupuy Smith, M.S. Ed.

Author

Robert Smith

Teacher Created Materials, Inc.
6421 Industry Way
Westminster, CA 92683

www.teachercreated.com
Reprinted, 2002
ISBN-1-57690-957-3

©2002 Teacher Created Materials, Inc.
Made in U.S.A.

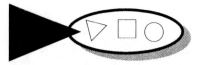

Table of Contents

A Note to Teachers and Parents

The design of this book is intended to be used by teachers or parents for a variety of purposes and needs.

The material in this book provides a broad range of experiences in geometry for students in the third through fifth grade years. Students will become familiar with plane and solid geometric figures. They will be familiar with the tools of geometry. They will know how to compute area and perimeter and recognize specific features of these figures.

Because there are clear, simple, and readable instruction pages for each unit, the book may be used as a formal instruction tool for teaching geometry. Capable readers could do the units with little or no math instruction and may occasionally need to clarify a specific concept.

This book could also be used in whole-class directed teaching instruction with the teacher or parent going page by page through the book. This book is organized to cover geometric topics sequentially. By following the organization of the book, teachers will cover a very wide range of geometric concepts in a sensible and workable way.

Teachers may choose to select units or concepts where additional help is needed by the class, by a group of students, or by individuals. Each unit is capable of standing on its own as an instructional tool for individual topics.

Teachers and parents working with children who are relatively new to the concepts may want to use a more gradual pace. A teacher may want to have two tracks within the class with one track moving at a faster pace and the other at a gradual pace—with the tempo appropriate to the abilities and backgrounds of individual students. The organization of the text also lends itself to use by a small group doing independent enrichment or advanced math. It is effective for individual or center activity.

If students get stuck on a specific concept or unit within this book, review the material and allow students to redo the pages that are giving them difficulty. Students should be allowed to use a calculator to check the accuracy of their work. This reduces the need for correction and allows the material to be self-corrected if that method works with students.

This book is designed to match the suggestions of the National Council for the Teachers of Mathematics. Use every opportunity to have students apply these new skills in classroom situations and at home. This will reinforce the value of the skills as well as the process.

This book matches many of the NCTM standards including these main topics and specific features.

Geometry

The geometry exercises in this book help students to identify, classify, compare, and describe geometric figures. Students will gain practice and skill in using the tools of geometry, such as the compass and protractor. Students learn to understand geometric relationships and properties, such as similarity, congruence, and symmetry, and to relate geometry to the physical world and to their personal experiences.

Measurement

This book encourages and guides the use of measuring tools and the development of the actual processes of measurement as they relate to length, area, perimeter, diameter, circumference, and angle. The text emphasizes practical applications for everyday living.

Mathematics as Problem Solving

This book offers opportunities to apply math skills in word-problem formats, to investigate and understand mathematical content, and to develop and apply problem-solving strategies. Students will also develop facility and confidence in their computational ability and their ability to apply mathematics meaningfully.

Mathematical Connections

The problems in this book help students see how mathematical ideas are related. Students will explore problems and describe results in geometric terms. Students recognize the use of mathematics in their daily lives at school, in the general culture, and in society.

Computation and Estimation

This book helps students use estimation to determine the reasonableness of an answer. They explore ways to use the arithmetic processes with many computations and word problems.

Other Standards

This book also aligns well with other standards which are concerned with communication in mathematics and recognizing and extending geometric patterns. The problems in this book help students understand and apply reasoning processes, especially as they apply to geometric concepts.

Facts to Know

Naming Angles

The direction an angle faces does not affect its name.

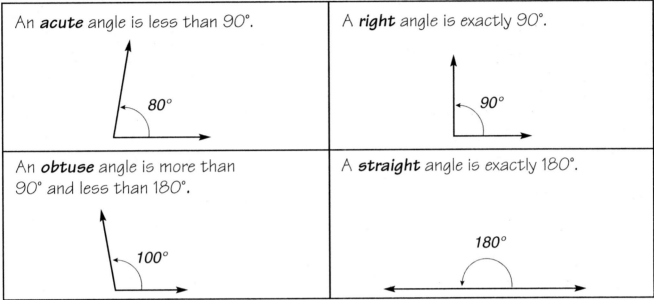

An **acute** angle is less than 90°. 80°	A **right** angle is exactly 90°. 90°
An **obtuse** angle is more than 90° and less than 180°. 100°	A **straight** angle is exactly 180°. 180°

A *protractor* is used to measure the exact size of an angle in terms of the number of degrees between 0° and 180°.

There are usually two sets of numbers on a protractor—one set running from left to right and the other set from right to left.

These two sets of numbers make it easy to line up the protractor on any angle.

The half-way point of every protractor is 90°. It is usually written once.

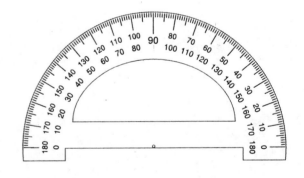

How to Use a Protractor

To measure an angle with a protractor, do the following steps.

1. Put the dot or circle at the center-bottom of the protractor directly on the point of the angle where the two rays meet. This point is called the vertex.
2. Carefully line up the black lines to the left or right of the circle along the bottom ray of the angle.
3. Determine where the top ray of the angle crosses the numbers on the protractor.
4. Determine if the angle is acute, obtuse, right, or straight.
5. Decide which set of numbers (inner or outer) fits this angle.

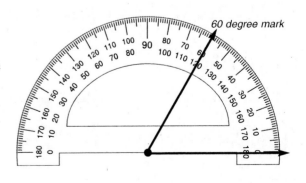

60 degree mark

Directions: Using the information on page 5, label each of the angles below as *acute*, *right*, *obtuse*, or *straight* angles.

1.

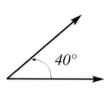

_____

2.

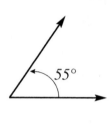

_____

3.

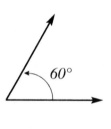

_____

4.

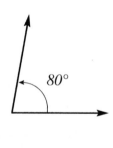

_____

5.

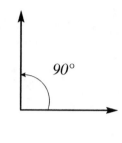

_____

6.

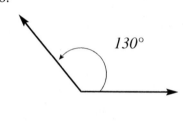

_____

7.

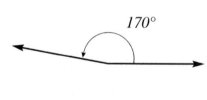

_____

8.

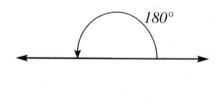

_____

Directions: Use a protractor and the information on page 5 to measure each of the angles below. Write the number of degrees on the first line and the name of each angle on the second line: *acute, right, obtuse,* or *straight.*

1.

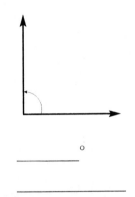

_____ °

_____

2.

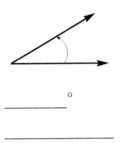

_____ °

_____

3.

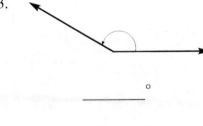

_____ °

_____

4.

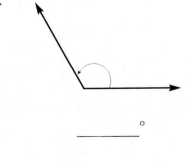

_____ °

_____

5.

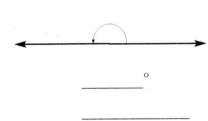

_____ °

_____

6.

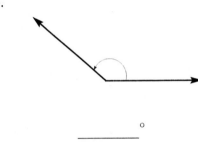

_____ °

_____

7.

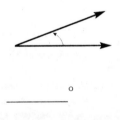

_____ °

_____

8.

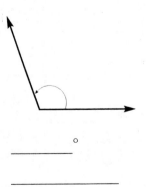

_____ °

_____

1 Practice ••••••••••••• Measuring More Angles with a Protractor

Directions: Use a protractor and the information on page 5 to make each of the angles indicated below. Write the name of each angle: *acute*, *right*, *obtuse*, or *straight*. One ray is drawn for you.

1. 30° ____________

2. 55° ____________

3. 90° ____________

4. 50° ____________

5. 100° ____________

6. 125° ____________

7. 160° ____________

8. 70° ____________

Facts to Know

- A **right** triangle has one 90° angle.

- An **equilateral** triangle has three equal sides and three equal angles of 60° each.

- An **isosceles** triangle has two equal sides and two equal angles.

- A **scalene** triangle has no equal sides and no equal angles.

- An **isosceles right** triangle has one 90° angle and two 45° angles. The sides adjacent (next to) the right angle are equal.

- An **acute** triangle has all three angles less than 90°.

- An **obtuse** triangle has one angle greater than 90°.

Note: Triangles can have more than one name.

Computing the Angles of a Triangle

- The sum of the interior angles of every triangle is 180°.

- If you know two of the angles of a triangle, you can find the third angle by adding the two angles you know and subtracting the sum from 180°.

This triangle has a 90° angle and a 60° angle.

$$\begin{array}{r} 90° \\ + 60° \\ \hline 150° \end{array} \qquad \begin{array}{r} 180° \\ - 150° \\ \hline 30° \end{array}$$

The remaining angle is 30°.

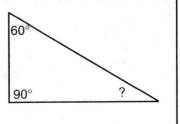

Measuring Angles with a Protractor

You can measure the angles of a triangle with a protractor using the same method you learned on page 5.

Directions: Use the information on page 9 to help you identify the name of each triangle below. If the triangle has more than one name, use all names.

1.

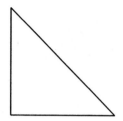

_____

2.

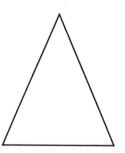

_____

3.

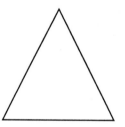

_____

4.

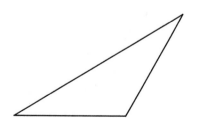

_____

5.

_____

6.

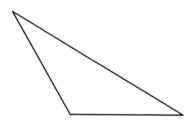

_____

7.

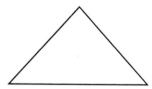

_____

8.

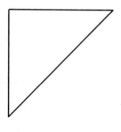

_____

Directions: Use the information on page 9 to help you determine the number of degrees in each unmarked angle below.

1.

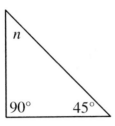

∠ n = _____

5.

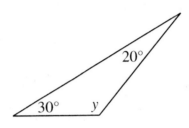

∠ y = _____

2.

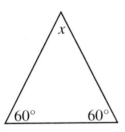

∠ x = _____

6.

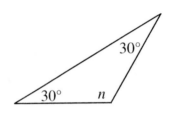

∠ n = _____

3.

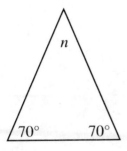

∠ n = _____

7.

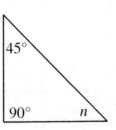

∠ n = _____

4.

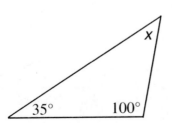

∠ x = _____

8.

∠ a = _____

Directions: Use a protractor and the information on pages 5 and 9 to help you measure each angle of the triangles on this page. Remember, the sum of all three angles should equal 180°.

> **Sample**
>
> ∠BAC = 60°
>
> ∠ACB = 90°
>
> ∠CBA = 45°
>
>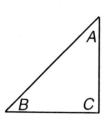
>
> **Note:** The middle letter indicates the point of the angle.

1.

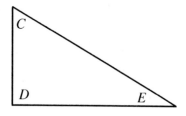

∠CDE = _____°

∠DEC = _____°

∠ECD = _____°

4.

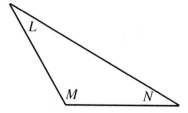

∠LMN = _____°

∠NLM = _____°

∠MNL = _____°

2.

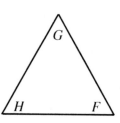

∠GHF = _____°

∠FGH = _____°

∠HFG = _____°

5.

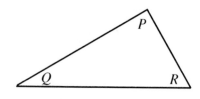

∠PQR = _____°

∠RPQ = _____°

∠QRP = _____°

3.

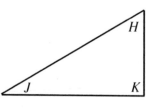

∠HJK = _____°

∠KHJ = _____°

∠JKH = _____°

6.

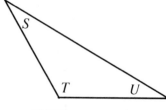

∠STU = _____°

∠UST = _____°

∠TUS = _____°

Facts to Know

> A *polygon* is a flat shape entirely enclosed by three or more straight sides.
> Polygons are named by the number of sides and angles they have.
> A *regular polygon* is one in which all sides are equal and all angles are equal.
> An *irregular polygon* does not have equal sides and equal angles.

Regular Polygons

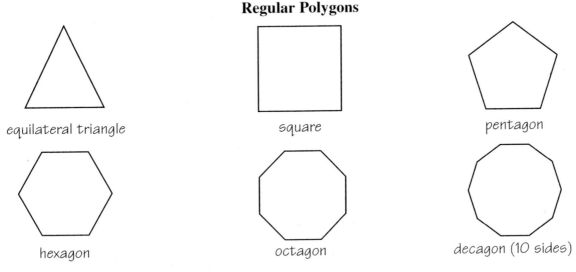

equilateral triangle   square   pentagon

hexagon   octagon   decagon (10 sides)

Different Types of Quadrilaterals

> A *quadrilateral* is a polygon that has 4 sides.
> The interior angles of a quadrilateral always add up to 360°.

rectangle   parallelogram   rhombus

trapezoid   isosceles trapezoid   kite

> All squares are also rectangles.
> All rectangles have four right angles (90°).
> All rectangles are also parallelograms because they have 2 pairs of parallel sides.
> All rhombuses are also parallelograms because they have two pairs of parallel sides.
> Some quadrilaterals with unequal sides have no specific name.

Measuring Angles in a Polygon

You can measure each interior angle in any polygon with a protractor.

Directions: Use the information on page 13 to help you identify each of the polygons below. Use the most specific name for each figure.

1.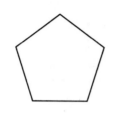

_____

2.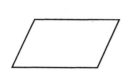

_____

3.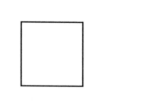

_____

4.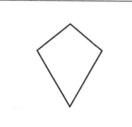

_____

5.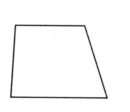

_____

6.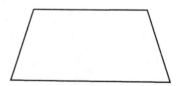

_____

7.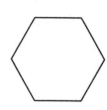

_____

8.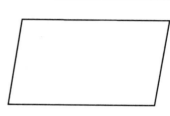

_____

9.

_____

10.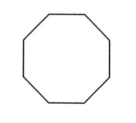

_____

11.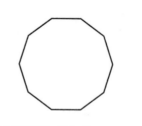

_____

12.

_____

Directions: Use a protractor and the information on pages 9 and 13 to measure each angle in the quadrilaterals on this page.

> **Sample**
>
> The interior angles of a quadrilateral always add up to 360°.
>
>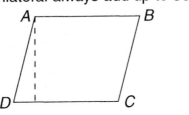
>
> ∠ABC = 75°
> ∠BCD = 105°
> ∠CDA = 75°
> ∠DAB = 105°

1.

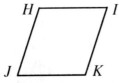

∠CDE = _____
∠DEF = _____
∠EFC = _____
∠FCD = _____

5.

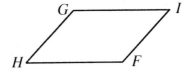

∠GHF = _____
∠HFI = _____
∠FIG = _____
∠IGH = _____

2.

∠HJK = _____
∠JKI = _____
∠KIH = _____
∠IHJ = _____

6.

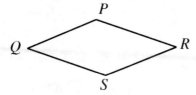

∠LMN = _____
∠MNO = _____
∠NOL = _____
∠OLM = _____

3.

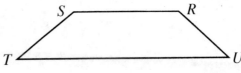

∠PQS = _____
∠QSR = _____
∠SRP = _____
∠RPQ = _____

7.

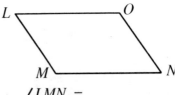

∠STU = _____
∠TUR = _____
∠URS = _____
∠RST = _____

4.

∠VXY = _____
∠XYW = _____
∠YWV = _____
∠WVX = _____

8.

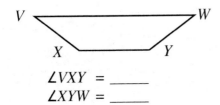

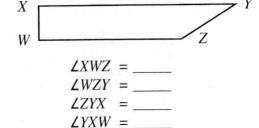

∠XWZ = _____
∠WZY = _____
∠ZYX = _____
∠YXW = _____

Directions: Use a protractor and the information in pages 9 and 13 to measure each angle in the polygons on this page.

1.

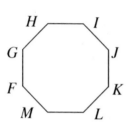

∠CDE = _____   ∠FAB = _____

∠DEF = _____   ∠ABC = _____

∠EFA = _____   ∠BCD = _____

4.

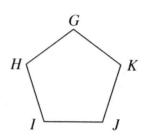

∠GKJ = _____   ∠IHG = _____

∠KJI = _____   ∠HGK = _____

∠JIH = _____

2.

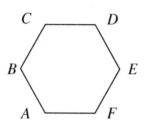

∠HIJ = _____   ∠LMF = _____

∠IJK = _____   ∠MFG = _____

∠JKL = _____   ∠FGH = _____

∠KLM = _____   ∠GHI = _____

∠QTU = _____

5.

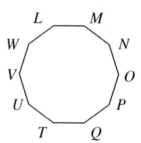

∠MNO = _____   ∠TUV = _____

∠NOP = _____   ∠UVW = _____

∠OPQ = _____   ∠VWL = _____

∠PQT = _____   ∠WLM = _____

3.

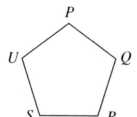

∠PQR = _____   ∠SUP = _____

∠QRS = _____   ∠UPQ = _____

∠RSU = _____

6.

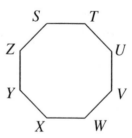

∠STU = _____   ∠WXY = _____

∠TUV = _____   ∠XYZ = _____

∠UVW = _____   ∠YZS = _____

∠VWX = _____   ∠ZST = _____

Facts to Know

The perimeter of a geometric figure is the distance around the figure.

Perimeter can be computed by adding the lengths of all the sides of the figure.

Perimeter of Squares

The perimeter of a square can be computed by multiplying the length of one side of the square by 4.

Each side of this square is 5 feet long. The perimeter is 4 x 5 feet or 20 feet.

5 ft.

Perimeter of Rectangles

The perimeter of a rectangle can be computed when you know the lengths of 2 adjacent sides (sides next to each other) of the rectangle.

The width of this rectangle is 4 inches and the length is 11 inches.

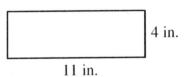

4 in.

11 in.

The formula for computing the perimeter of the rectangle is:

$P = (l + w)$ x 2 or $P = 2l + 2w$ or $P = 2(11$ in.$) + 2(4$ in.$) = 30$ in.

The perimeter is computed by adding the length plus the width and multiplying the sum times two.

Perimeter of Parallelograms

The perimeter of any parallelogram can be computed using the same formula used for a rectangle.

$P = (l + w)$ x 2 or $P = 2l + 2w$

$P = (10 + 6)$ x 2

$P = 32$ ft.

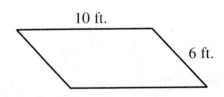

10 ft.

6 ft.

Perimeter of Irregular Quadrilaterals

The perimeter of figures with 4 unequal sides is computed by adding the lengths of each side.

Perimeter of Regular Polygons

A regular polygon is a polygon that has equal sides and equal angles.

The perimeter of a regular polygon is computed by multiplying the length of one side by the number of sides.

P = number of sides x 5

$P = 5$ x 6

$P = 30$

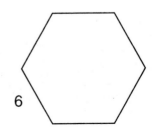

6

Directions: Use the information on page 17 to help you compute the perimeter of a square with each dimension.

1. s = 8 ft.

    P = _____

3. s = 10 m

    P = _____

2. s = 12 cm

    P = _____

4. s = 7 in.

    P = _____

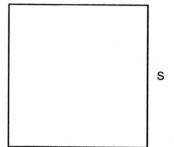

Directions: Use the information on page 17 to help you compute the perimeter of a rectangle with each set of dimensions.

5. l = 12 m

    w = 5 m

    P = _____

7. l = 9 in.

    w = 16 in.

    P = _____

6. l = 15 ft.

    w = 10 ft.

    P = _____

8. l = 20 yd.

    w = 12 yd.

    P = _____

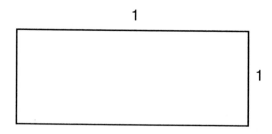

Directions: Use the information on page 17 to help you compute the perimeter of a parallelogram with each set of dimensions.

9. l = 22 ft.

    w = 20 ft.

    P = _____

11. l = 17 in.

    w = 12 in.

    P = _____

10. l = 40 cm

    w = 16 cm

    P = _____

12. l = 11 yd.

    w = 19 yd.

    P = _____

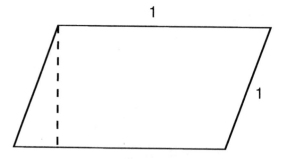

Directions: Use the information below and on page 17 to help you compute the perimeter of the following quadrilaterals.

The perimeter of figures with four unequal sides is computed by adding the lengths of each side.

7 ft. + 4 ft. + 9 ft. + 5 ft. = 25 ft.

The perimeter of this quadrilateral is 25 ft.

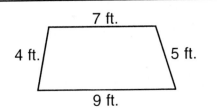

1.

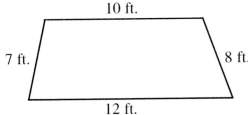

P = _____

2.

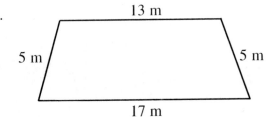

P = _____

3.

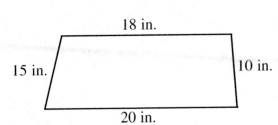

P = _____

4.

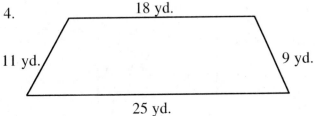

P = _____

5.

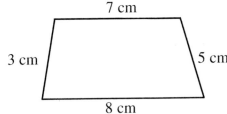

P = _____

6.

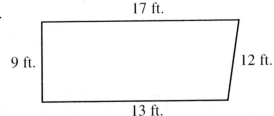

P = _____

7.

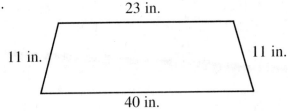

P = _____

8.

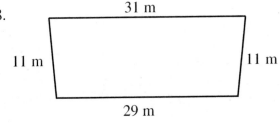

P = _____

Directions: Use the information below and on page 17 to help you compute the perimeter of these regular polygons.

> **Sample**
> This regular hexagon has 6 equal sides.
> Each side is 7 in. long.
> P = number of sides x 7 in.
> The perimeter is 6 x 7 in. or 42 in.
>
> 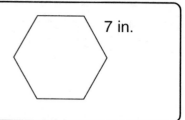 7 in.

1.
9 in.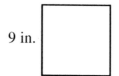

P = _____

5.
20 ft.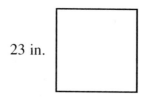

P = _____

2.
13 ft.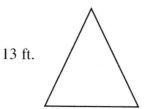

P = _____

6.
23 in.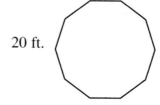

P = _____

3.
10 m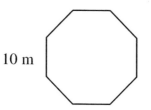

P = _____

7.
35 cm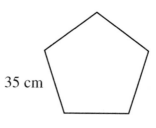

P = _____

4.
12 yd.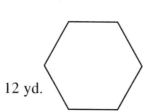

P = _____

8.
17 m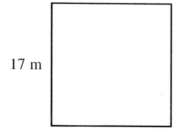

P = _____

Facts to Know

The *area* of a flat surface is a measure of how much space is covered by that surface. Area is measured in square units.

Square Area

Look at the rectangle drawn here. Notice that it is covered with 8 square tiles. The area of the rectangle is 8 square tiles.

The width of one side is 3 tiles and the length of the other side is 8 tiles. The area is 24 square tiles.

The area of a rectangle is equal to length times width.

The formula is: $A = l \times w$

Graph Paper Area

Count the number of squares along the width of the rectangle.

Count the number of squares along the length of the rectangle.

Multiply the answers.

Count the number of squares in this rectangle.

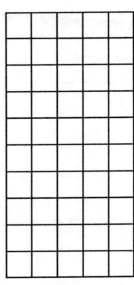

> $A = l \times w$
>
> $A = 10 \times 5$
>
> $A = 50$

The area of this rectangle is 50 square units.

5 Practice ••••••••••••••••• Computing Areas of Geometric Shapes

Directions: Cut out the square units below. Use them to compute the area for each of the following rectangles.

1.

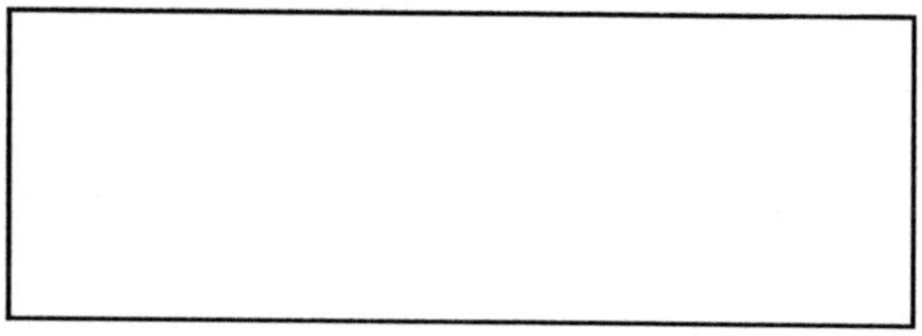

l = _______ units w = _______ units

A = ___________

2.

l = _______ units w = _______ units

A = ___________

3.

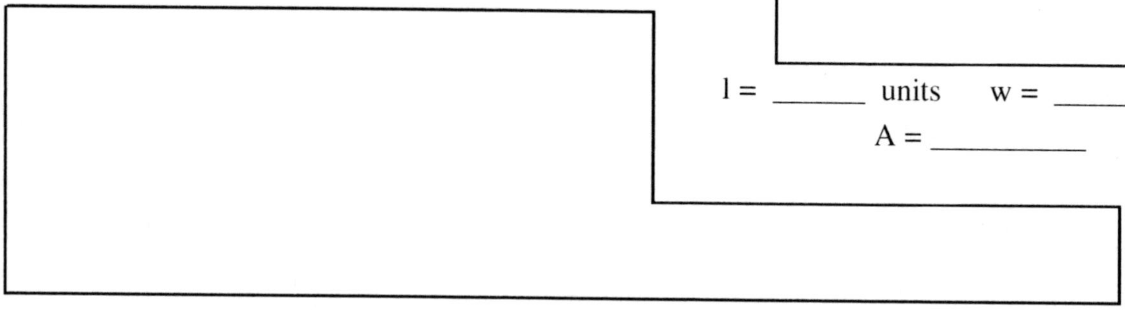

A = ___________

4.

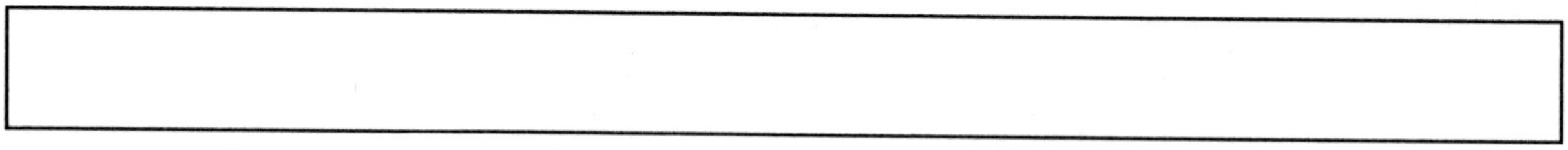

l = _______ units w = _______units A = ___________

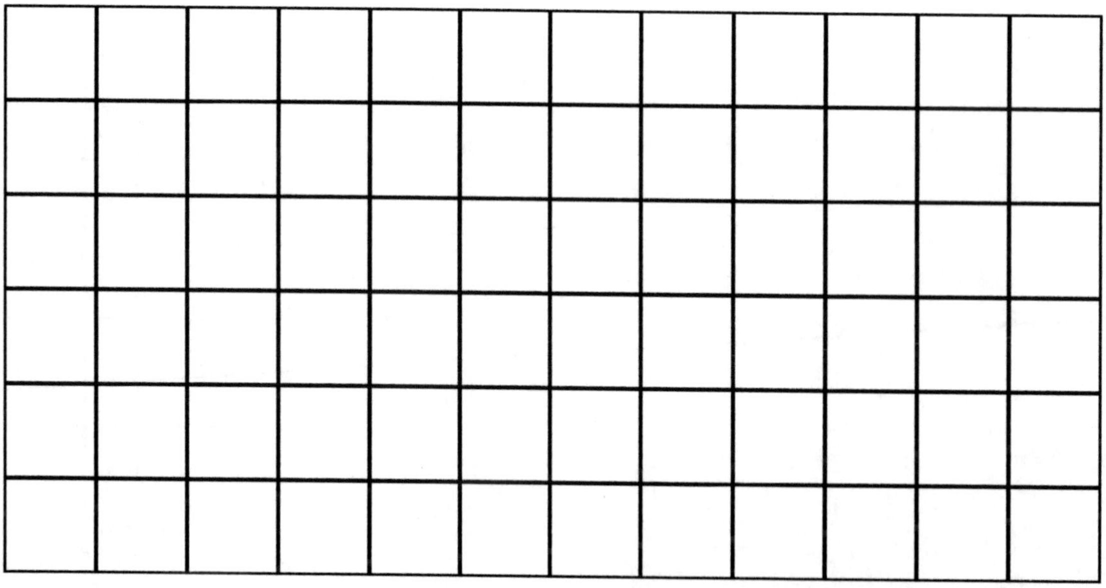

The rectangle drawn on this graph paper is 3 squares wide and 11 spaces long.

The area is 33 square units.

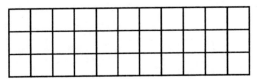

Directions: Use the information on page 21 to help you compute the area of each rectangle.

1.

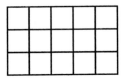

A = _____ square units

5.

A = _____ square units

2.

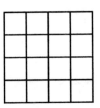

A = _____ square units

6.

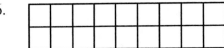

A = _____ square units

3.

A = _____ square units

7.

A = _____ square units

4.

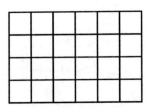

A = _____ square units

8.

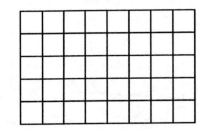

A = _____ square units

       #2957 How to Succeed in Geometry: Grades 3–5

Directions: Compute the number of square centimeters (cm) in these figures.

1.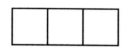

_____ cm²

3.

_____ cm²

2.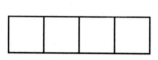

_____ cm²

4.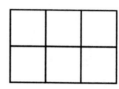

_____ cm²

Directions: Use the square inch to determine the area of these rectangular figures.

5.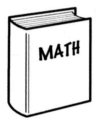

a math book cover

_____ in.²

8.

a tissue

_____ in.²

6.

one sheet of paper

_____ in.²

9.

a ruler

_____ in.²

7.

a paperback book cover

_____ in.²

10.

a binder cover

_____ in.²

Facts to Know

The area of a flat surface is a measure of how much space is covered by that surface. Area is measured in square units.

Area of a Square

The area of a square is computed by multiplying the length of one side times itself.

$A = s \times s$ or $A = s^2$ (Area = side squared)

The square shown here has 4 units on each side.

$A = 4 \times 4$

$A = 16$ square units

4

Area of a Rectangle

The area of a rectangle is computed by multiplying the width of one side times the length of the adjoining side.

$A = l \times w$

The rectangle shown here has 9 units on one side and 4 units on the adjoining side.

$A = 9 \times 4$

$A = 36$ square units

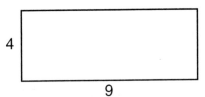

4

9

Note: The area of a rectangle can also be determined by multiplying the base times the height.

Area of a Parallelogram

The area of a parallelogram is computed by multiplying the base times the height.

$A = b \times h$

$A = 4 \times 9$

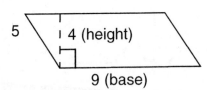

5   ⌐ 4 (height)
⌐
9 (base)

This parallelogram has a base of 8 units and a height of 4 units.

$A = 8 \times 4$

$A = 32$ square units

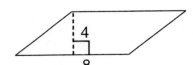

4

8

Area of a Triangle

A triangle is always one half of a rectangle or a parallelogram.

The area of a triangle is computed by multiplying 1/2 times the base times the height of the triangle.

$A = 1/2 \; b \times h$

$A = 1/2 \times 6 \times 8$

$A = 24$ square units

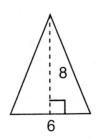

8

6

Directions: Use the information on page 25 to compute the area of the squares below.

1.   6 in.

_____

2.   10 ft.

_____

3.   12 m

_____

4.   30 cm

_____

5.   15 in.

_____

6.   23 m

_____

7.   25 yd.

_____

8.   41 ft.

_____

Remember these formulas.

Area of a rectangle = length times width or base times height

$A = l \times w$ or $A = b \times h$

Area of a parallelogram = base times height

$A = b \times h$

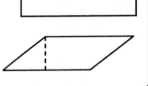

Directions: Use the information above and on page 25 to compute the area of the following rectangles.

Directions: Use the information above and on page 25 to compute the area of the following parallelograms.

1.

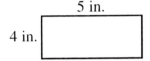

5 in.

4 in.

A = _____

2.

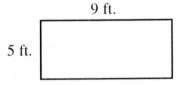

9 ft.

5 ft.

A = _____

3.

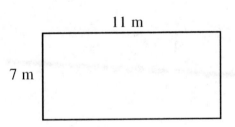

11 m

7 m

A = _____

4.

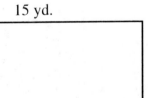

15 yd.

6 yd.

A = _____

5.

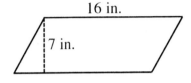

16 in.

7 in.

A = _____

6.

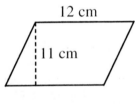

12 cm

11 cm

A = _____

7.

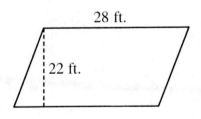

28 ft.

22 ft.

A = _____

8.

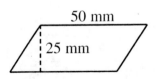

50 mm

25 mm

A = _____

Remember: The area of a triangle is one half the area of a parallelogram or a rectangle. It is 1/2 the base times the height.

$A = 1/2\ b \times h$

This triangle has a height of 6 inches and a base of 10 inches.

The area is 1/2 x 10 x 6 or 30 in.²

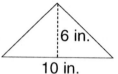

6 in.

10 in.

Directions: Use the information above and on page 25 to compute the area of the following triangles.

1.

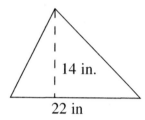

14 in.

22 in

A = _____

5.

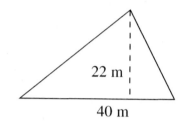

22 m

40 m

A = _____

2.

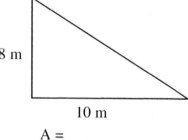

8 m

10 m

A = _____

6.

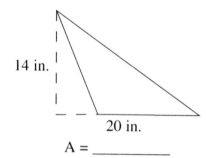

14 in.

20 in.

A = _____

3.

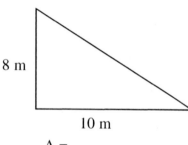

14 yd.

20 yd.

A = _____

7.

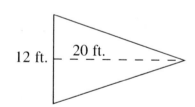

12 ft.   20 ft.

A = _____

4.

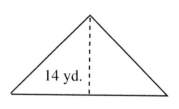

9 cm

16 cm

A = _____

8.

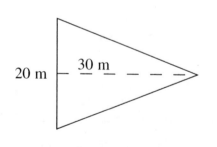

20 m   30 m

A = _____

Facts to Know

A compass can be used to divide a circle into exactly six equal sections.

Rule of Six

1. Set the compass setting to the exact length of the radius of the circle by placing the compass point on the center point of the circle and the pencil point exactly on the circle.
2. Make a point on the circle and label it A.
3. Don't change the compass setting. Place the compass point on A and draw an arc on the circle.
4. Label point B where the arc crosses the circle.
5. Don't change the compass setting. Place the compass point on B and draw another arc on the circle.
6. Label point C where the arc crosses the circle.
7. Don't change the compass setting. Place the compass point on C and draw another arc on the circle.
8. Label point D where the arc crosses the circle.
9. Don't change the compass setting. Place the compass point on D and draw another arc on the circle.
10. Label point E where the arc crosses the circle.
11. Don't change the compass setting. Place the compass point on E and draw another arc on the circle.
12. Label point F where the arc crosses the circle.

Check Your Work

Place the compass point on F and draw another arc on the circle.

If the arc goes directly through point A, you did it exactly right.

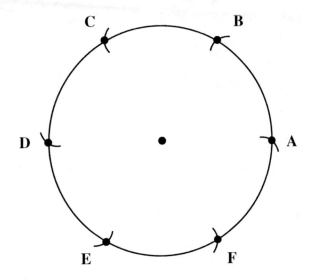

Directions: Use the Rule of Six, on each circle below, as show on page 29. Inscribe an equilateral triangle in each circle as show in the first problem.

Directions: Use the Rule of Six to make six equal sections in the circle. Then, inscribe two equilateral triangles using the points.

1.

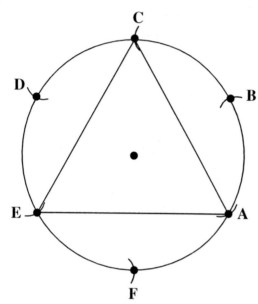

4.

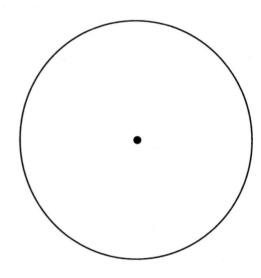

2.

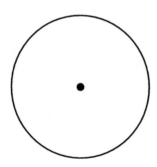

5.

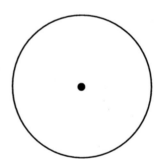

3.

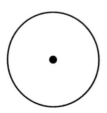

Directions: Use the Rule of Six, on each circle below, as shown on page 29. Inscribe a regular hexagon in each circle as shown in the first problem

1.

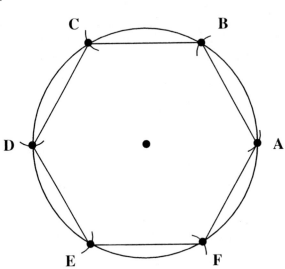

4.

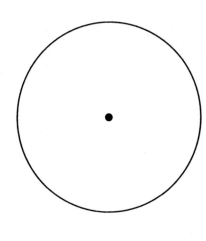

2.

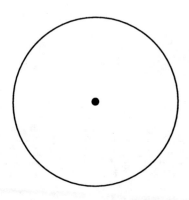

5.

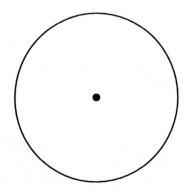

3.

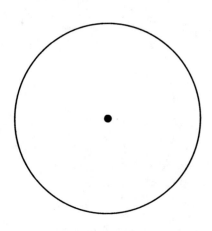

6.

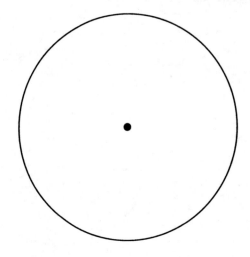

#2957 How to Succeed in Geometry: Grades 3–5

Facts to Know

You can inscribe a square within a circle this way:

1. Draw a straight line through the center of the circle.
2. Label this diameter AB.
3. Make the compass longer than radius AO. It can be a little longer or a lot longer.
4. Place the compass point on point A and draw an arc above the diameter and an arc below the diameter.
5. Don't change the setting. Place the compass point on point B and draw an intersecting arc above the diameter and an arc below the diameter.
6. Draw a straight line through the two points of intersection and point O.
7. Label points C and D where the line crosses the circle.
8. Connect point A to point C. Connect point C to point B. Connect point B to point D. Connect point D to point A. The square is now finished.

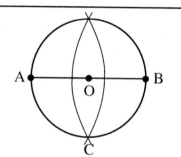

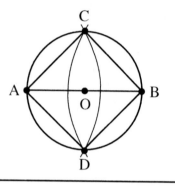

Directions: Use the information above to inscribe a square in each of the following circles.

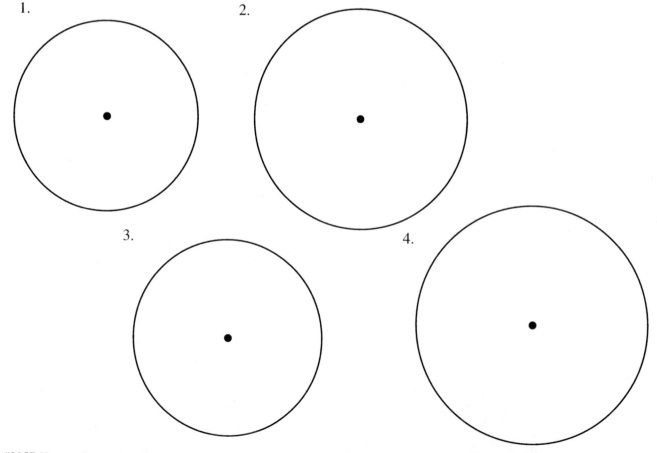

1.

2.

3.

4.

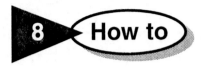
Facts to Know

Symmetry

A line of symmetry is a line drawn through the center of a flat shape so that one half of the shape can be folded to fit exactly over the other half.

These figures show 1 line of symmetry.

These figures show more than one line of symmetry.

    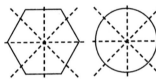

These figures show no lines of symmetry.

    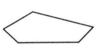

Congruence

- Congruent figures fit exactly over each other.
- Congruent figures are exactly the same in shape and size.
- Congruent figures can be turned over or around to fit.

congruent triangles   **congruent parallelograms**

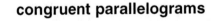
  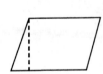 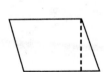

Similar

- Similar figures are the same in shape but different in size.
- One similar figure is larger than the other.
- The corresponding angles in each similar figure will be equal.

similar triangles   **similar parallelograms**

   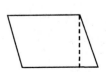

Directions: Use the information on page 33 to draw one line of symmetry through the figures below. Circle the figures that have no line of symmetry.

1.

2.

3.

4.

5.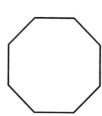

6.

Directions: Use the information on page 33 to draw two or more lines of symmetry through the figures below.

7.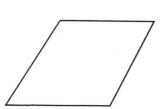

8.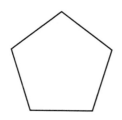

9.

10.

11.

12.

13.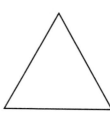

14.

Directions: Use the information on page 33 to determine which of the figures in each of the following sets are congruent. Cross out the letters of the congruent figures.

1.

 A B C D

2.

 A B C 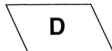 D

3.

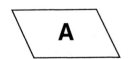 A B C 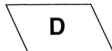 D

4.

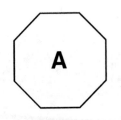 A 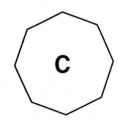 B 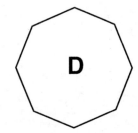 C 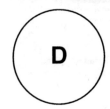 D

5.

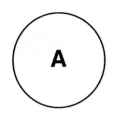 A 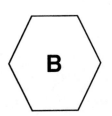 B 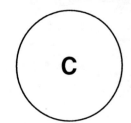 C 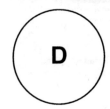 D

6.

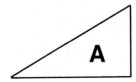 A B 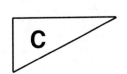 C D

Directions: Use the information on page 33 to determine which of the figures in each set below are similar. Cross out the letters of the similar figures.

1.

   D

2.

3.

   D

Directions: Determine which figures in each set are similar and which are congruent.

4. similar _____

   congruent _____

  C

5. similar _____

   congruent _____

   D

6. similar _____

   congruent _____

Facts to Know

- There are only 5 regular geometric solids or polyhedrons.
- The faces of each regular polyhedron are congruent.
- The faces are always regular polyhedrons.
- The edges of each regular polyhedron are identical.
- The vertices of each regular polyhedron are identical.
- The angles of each regular polyhedron are identical.
- These are sometimes called the 5 platonic solids.

tetrahedron octahedron hexahedron

dodecahedron icosahedron

Faces, Edges, and Vertices

- A face is the flat surface of a three-dimensional figure.
- An edge is a line segment where two faces meet.
- A vertex is the point where edges meet.

edge

vertex ——— face

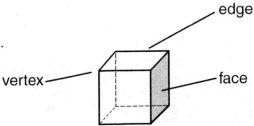

Other Geometric Solids

rectangular prism   triangular prism   cone   sphere

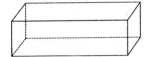

cylinder   square pyramid   triangular pyramid

Directions: Use the information on page 37 to identify each of these figures.

1. _____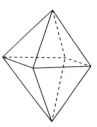

2. _____

3. _____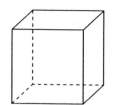

4. _____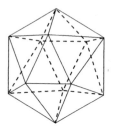

5. _____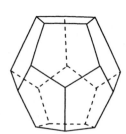

6. _____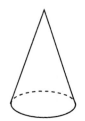

7. _____

8. _____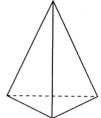

9. _____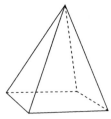

10. _____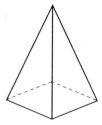

11. _____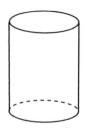

12. _____

Directions: Count the number of faces, edges, and vertices for each geometric solid on this page. Name each solid.

1.

name _____

faces_____

edges _____

vertices _____

2.

name _____

faces_____

edges _____

vertices _____

3.

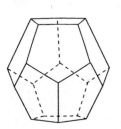

name _____

faces_____

edges _____

vertices _____

4.

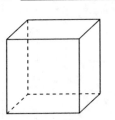

name _____

faces_____

edges _____

vertices _____

5.

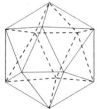

name _____

faces _____

edges _____

vertices _____

6.

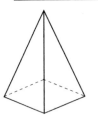

name _____

faces _____

edges _____

vertices _____

7.

name _____

faces _____

edges _____

vertices _____

8.

name _____

faces _____

edges _____

vertices _____

9 Practice ••••• Euler's Formula with Polyhedrons

The following chart contains other polyhedra. Can you use Euler's formula to determine the number of faces (F), vertices (V), and edges (E) for each figure? Fill in the chart.

Euler's Formula: $F + V - 2 = E$

Polyhedron	Faces	Vertices	Edges
pentahedron 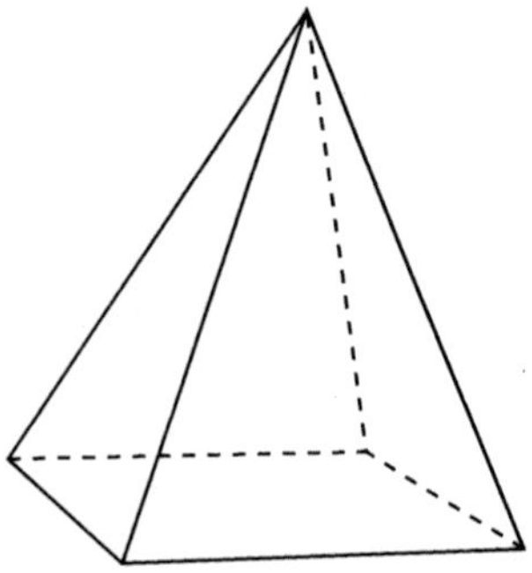			
decahedron 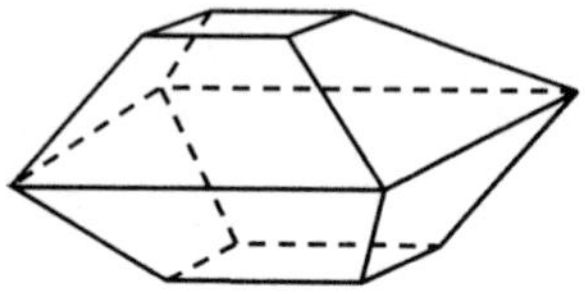			
heptahedron 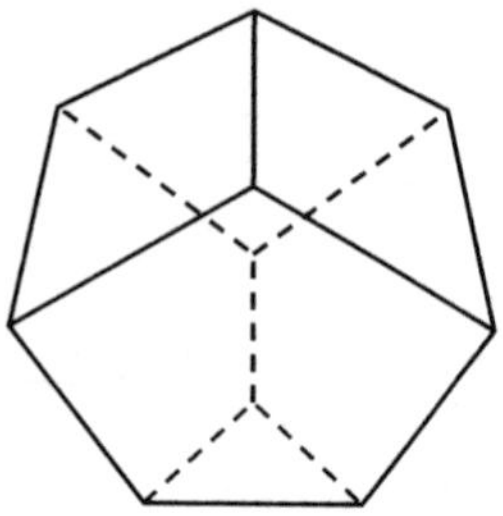			

Facts to Know

- The *circumference* (C) is the distance around a circle. It is the perimeter of a circle.
- The *radius* (r) is the distance from the center of a circle to any point on the circle.
- A *chord* is a line segment connecting any two points on a circle.
- The longest possible chord is a diameter.
- The *diameter* (d) is a line segment extending from one side of the circle to the other through the center of the circle.

Directions: Label the circumference, the radius, the diameter, and a chord on each circle below. The first circle has been done as an example.

1.

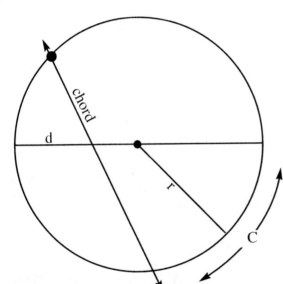

3.

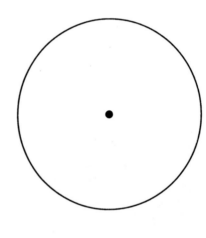

2.

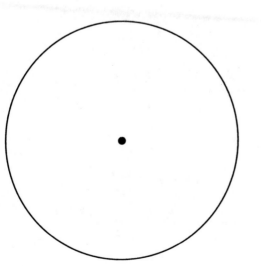

4.

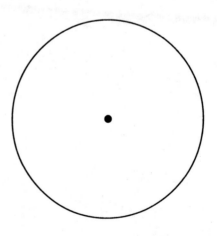

Facts to Know

- You can draw an infinite (unlimited) number of radii in a circle.
- You can draw an infinite (unlimited) number of diameters in a circle.
- The diameter is always twice the length of a radius ($d = 2r$).
- The radius is always one half of the diameter ($r = \frac{d}{2}$).
- The circumference is a little more than 3 times the length of the diameter.

Directions: Give the length of the radius and diameter for each circle shown. Give an estimated value for the circumference by multiplying 3 times the diameter.

1.

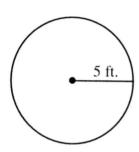

5 ft.

r = _____
d = _____
C = _____

4.

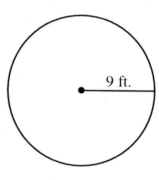

9 ft.

r = _____
d = _____
C = _____

2.

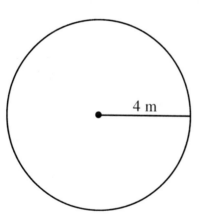

4 m

r = _____
d = _____
C = _____

5.

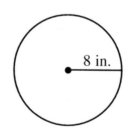

8 in.

r = _____
d = _____
C = _____

3.

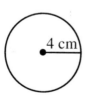

4 cm

r = _____
d = _____
C = _____

6.

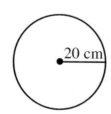

20 cm

r = _____
d = _____
C = _____

Facts to Know

A *tessellation* is a repeated pattern using geometric figures that cover a surface entirely. There are no spaces between the figures. This tessellation is made with equilateral triangles.

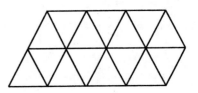

Directions: Use the figures to extend the tessellations shown below by outlining the figures as often as you can in the space provided.

equilateral triangle	square	rectangle	isosceles right triangle

 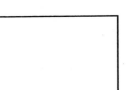

1. equilateral triangle tessellation

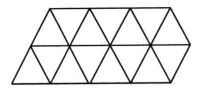

2. square tessellation

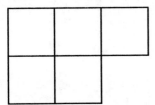

3. equilateral triangle and square tessellation

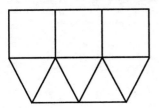

4. isosceles right triangle tessellation

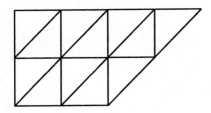

Facts to Know

A regular hexagon will always create a tessellating pattern. So will an equilateral triangle or a rectangle.

Directions: Use the hexagon and the figures from page 43 to extend the tessellations shown below by outlining the figures as often as you can in the space available.

1. hexagon tessellation

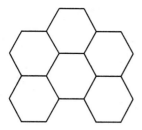

2. hexagon and equilateral triangle

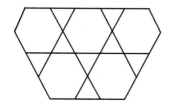

3. hexagon, equilateral triangle, and rectangle tessellation

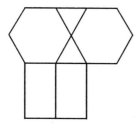

4. your own design (any combination of figures that works)